Mervin Evans

Funding

101

The Workbook

ISBN-13: 978-1508488668

ISBN-10: 1508488665

Why are you going to start this business?

Can You afford to leave your current employment for the next 12 months?

How will you support yourself?

What makes you special?

List five major business success stories

What Special Skills do you have?

What Marketing Skills do you have?

Why is there a need for your product or service in the marketplace?

Please compare yourself to another in the marketplace!

What business experience do you have?

Please provide an accounting of your last 10 years!

Have you worked with the Public before?

Describe your best and worst incidents?

Describe your history of Supervision?

What type of problems caused you the worst concerns?

What does your family think about this project?

Will your family invest?

Why Not?

Please describe current Financial Position.

Why are things the way they are?

Describe Your Personal Goals.

Outline a: 5, 10, 20 Year Life Plan!

WHAT IS YOUR EDUCATIONAL BACKGROUND?

Please list special training that supports this new business!

What is your history of Community Involvement?

What organizations do you belong to?

What would you do if this business fail?

What is your security to offset the funding
or investment capital?

How would you pay the Investor or Bank Back, if you failed?

How many months will it take and what detail plan will you follow?

What is the real market potential of this
business?

Describe your supporting data?

Describe the Ownership of the Business?

Is this a family based business?

Date of Incorporation?

State of Incorporation?

Legal Form of business   History of
Ownership

Describe past failures?

Cover Sheet of Funding Request

Name of Business:

Address:

City, State Zip

Phone:

Funding Requirements:

Type of Funding:

Statement of Purpose of Business

Why is there a need for this Business?

First Year Goals

First Month

First 90 Days

First 180 Days

Second and Third Year Goals

Third Year Benchmarks?

Table of Contents

Introduction

A

B

C

D

Conclusion

Appendix

Executive Summary - (5 Pages)

Management

Service/Product

Profit Centers

The Industry and Your Business

Growth Trends

Description of your Business

Operational Details

Hours of Service

What is your market?

Scope of Research

Who are your customers?

Social Factors?

Who is the Competition?

Local

State

National

What makes your business better than the Competition?

Why are you sure?

What is the location of the business?

What made you select this place?

From the customer point of view - "Why are you at this location? "

Please describe the research involved in selecting the location of the business?

Management Statements

Listings of key people

Key Personnel

Primary Staff

Support Staff

Use of Funds Statement

Short Term

Long Term

Start-up Funds needed?

Lowest possible Start-up budget

Highest desired Start-up Budget

Supporting Data

Capital Equipment needed

Computers Requirements?

Effect of Funding

Short Term

Long Term

Current Balance Sheet

Breakeven Analysis Statement

Supporting Data

Income Projections

Cash Flow Statement

What Research work that you have done so far?

Sources of Research Data

History of the Business from the Past Owners

Have you verified the data?

How did you verify the data?

Balance Sheet

Income Statement

TAX RETURNS Federal and State
(Business)

TAX RETURNS Federal and State
(Personal)

Personal Financial Statements

Principal # 1

Principal # 2

Principal # 3

Cost of living Statement

Principal # 1

Principal # 2

Principal # 3

Credit History

Principal # 1

Principal # 2

Principal # 3

List of References

Banker

Accountant

Attorney

Trade References

#1

#2

#3

Employment History

Current Employment

Past Employers

Principal # 1

Principal # 2

Principal # 3

Real Estate Agreements

Describe all contract and provide copies of all materials.

Contracts

Can we factor these contracts

List of Major Customers

How did you develop this list?

Letters of Intent from Major Customers

What is the dollar value of each major customer?

List of Major Suppliers

What is the Contract Value of
each major Supplier?

Letters of Intent from Major Suppliers

D & B or TRW Business Credit
Report on the top 5 Major Suppliers

Articles of Incorporation

Why did you incorporate?

DBA or Business Permits

What permits are still needed?

Closing Statements

Why is this a good investment?

Resume of General Manager

Education

Past Employment

Five Year Personal Goals

First Year

Second Year

Thir Year

Fourth Year

Fifth Year

Describe Credit Problems the Business may have.

What is your plan of action to solve these problems?

Your Company's Credit Policy

Term and Conditions of Credit?

Your Company's Collection Policy

Standards and Rating Policy

Employee Relationship

Contract Services

Company's need for Consulting Services

Services of Mervin Evans needed

MERVIN EVANS
Investor Video Script

Hello My Name is_____ YOUR NAME

I am the President of _____ Company Name

Do not give anyone any money unless you are in direct contact with me after you have gotten a written agreement and all of your questions are answered !

My Phone Number is _____

There is a High Degree of Risk involved in investing in new companies. This investment is not Approved by any State Department of Corporations or Federal Agency including the Securities Exchange Commission. Do not Invest any Retirement Income or Life Savings! Consult with your CPA and Attorney Prior to making any Investment. This Company is not listed on any Stock Exchange. Investors not capable of a 100% Loss Should not Consider this Investment.

We are looking for $_____ AMOUNT OF FUNDING REQUEST   We have an exciting company!

71

Our Vision / Mission Statement

In YEAR[xx], [Company] was [formed / created] to [describe the purpose of your activities]. Overall, our company can be characterized as a [x] (high-profile retail merchant, aggressive distributor or x, quality manufacturer of x--the business and image for your customers to see). Examples of purpose: produce or distribute [x], take advantage of [x], fill the void of [x] Include company vision and mission statements covering your line of products or services: What kind of company do you intend to be? What is your desired company image?

Objectives

Near term and long term---Revenue projected for fiscal year 19[xx] without external funding is expected to be $[x]. Annual growth is projected to be [x]% per year through 19[xx]. We feel that within [x] years [Company] will be in a suitable position for [further expansion, an initial public offering or profitable acquisition]. Our objective, at this time, is to propel the company into a prominent market position.

Background

For many years people have [x]. How people managed to do without [your product / service]. The "state of the art"/condition of the industry today is such that [x]. Explain your present situation in the industry vis-a-vis competition or technology, etc. How and where a similar product or service is now being used. Describe the [concept / opportunity / niche] in your marketplace to exploit as you build your business to the next level, etc. We have just started / completed the design / development / testing / introduction of (product / service) -- a novel and proprietary [x] (example: soap for cleaning vinyl, retail store, construction tool, etc.) The legal form of [Company] is [Sole Owner / General or Limited Partnership / Corporation / Subchapter S-Corporation], located in [list primary business address as well as satellite locations].

Capital Requirements

According to the opportunities and requirements for [Company] described in this business plan, and based on what we feel are sound business assumptions, our [initial / first year / total] capital requirements are for $[x] by [date], 19[xx]. To accomplish this goal we have developed a comprehensive plan to intensify and accelerate our marketing and sales activities, product development, services expansion, engineering, distribution and customer service. To implement our plans we require a [loan / investment] totaling $[x] for the following purposes:

Management Team

Our management team consists of [x] men and women whose backgrounds consist of [x] years of marketing with [list company names], and [x] years of corporate development with [list company names]. Our management team also includes [x] men and women with [x] years of engineering and design with [company], a chief financial officer with [x] years of accounting, administrative, merger and acquisition, banking experience with [company]. Strong company backgrounds pertinent to your management team's functions are good references to demonstrate a solid background and assure a higher probability of future success.

In-House Management

[x], President

[x], Vice President of Marketing

[x], Vice President of Sales

[x], Vice President of Finance

[x], Vice President of R&D

[x], Vice President of Operations

[x], Controller

Outside Management Support

[hourly / project basis]

[x], Accountant / CPA
[x], Corporate Attorney
[x], [Type of Consultant]

Conclusion

Thank You for Watching I look forward to getting with you soon

NAME - Position in Company

Phone   Mailing Address

MERVIN L. EVANS

Author: NEW YORK VENTURE CAPITAL DIRECTORY

About the Author

General Partner - EVANS VENTURE PARTNERS - CA LP 9121800010

Results - Relationships - Respected .

Mr. Evans hands on operations experience can help new business owners to overcome many obstacles. Evans Partners is looking for companies that have strong management, innovative product line and solid growth potential. Mervin Evans is a past Employee of the State of California, a major Bar Association. Evans has consulted a number of Superior Court Judges.

Evans manages all aspects of the fund raising process. Evans Partners believes in being a value-added investor, working in cooperation with management to build great companies and create shareholder value. Our partners have extensive experience in many areas relevant to the development and success of an early stage technology company, including research and development, production planning and operations, strategic planning, licensing and sourcing agreements, recruiting and human resource development, and finance.

Evans Venture Partners is differentiated by its commitment to early stage investing, its experience in working with and supporting emerging technology companies, and by its powerful international network which its partners can leverage on behalf of portfolio companies. Mervin Evans has a proven track record of doing just that for 12 years, and these skills and commitments are becoming increasingly important in today's global technology market.

BOOKS BY MERVIN EVANS

California Venture Capital Directory: California's Top Money Managers!

Credit Repair Made Easy

Evans Credit Workshop - How to Prepare and Present a Credit Request!

Evans Funding Workshop How to Prepare and Present a Venture Capital Funding Request!

Evans One Thousand Venture Capital Directory

New York Venture Capital Directory

Venture Capital Made Easy!

What Credit Reporting Agencies Don't Want You to Know

Mervin Evans Video

Most professional production companies are equipped to help with the planning of your video production. They have the resources and professional knowledge to help pull all of these elements together. When interviewing production companies, ask to see samples of work they have produced. Ask for references and follow up on those references to see how the company performed. Meet with the people that will be involved on the project. It is very important that you are comfortable and able to communicate with the people working on the project. Your Investor Video production will consist of three phases, pre-production, production and post-production. The pre-production phase is where the most time will have to be spent.

PO BOX 71351 Los Angeles CA 90071 323 301-0499 323-421-9436-FAX

RATE CARD - Video & Photography

1-Hour...$350

3-Hours..$500

6-Hours...$1,000

$350-Investor DVD 50 Copies
MERVIN EVANS   VIDEO...The Production Process

How to Approach a Venture Capitalist

Venture Capitalists are not untouchable people, but they are very busy. Telephone conversations should be friendly, but succinct and to the point. Many times the venture capitalist will require a review of your business plan before talking with you. Be willing to send your plan in advance of any conversation, and follow up on the stated date and time mentioned in your cover letter. There are many sources for venture capital and you as the entrepreneur should be willing to solicit several firms. The initial response time is usually several weeks, with the entire deal taking several months.   Venture capitalists typically expect a 20% to 50% annual return on their investment at the time they are bought out. Some will invest as little as $50,000 and as much as $20 million in any one company, but typical investments range from between $500,000 and $5 million. Management experience is a major consideration in evaluating financing prospects.

When producing a investor video there are a lot of things you have to consider. The following information will help you prepare yourself to make your production of a Investor DVD go smoothly. The first thing you have to plan is the business budget and the size of the funding request. Your business can not be ran on the cheap! The more time you put into planning and organizing your business, the more time and money you will save in the end. The average cost of production of a investor DVD can range from $250 to $1,500 per finished minute, we offer a flat rate quote of $350.

Most professional production companies are equipped to help with the planning of your video production. They have the resources and professional knowledge to help pull all of these elements together. When interviewing production companies, ask to see samples of work they have produced. Ask for references and follow up on those references to see how the company performed. Meet with the people that will be involved on the project. It is very important that you are comfortable and able to communicate with the people working on the project.   Your Investor Video production will consist of three phases, pre-production, production and post-production.   The pre-production phase is where the most time will have to be spent.

You must define a set of Goals for your business.   What are the Success and Management Issues? Who are the customers for the business?   Are you ready to start this business ?